Chasing the Cure

Written by
Doris Razo

ISBN No. 978-0-6152-3682-7

1st Edition

This book is dedicated to my daughters,
Natalie and Megan Calleros

A special thanks to my mother, Aurora, who threw me a lifesaver. To my dad, Eusebio, for giving me his strength and care. To my sisters, Blanca and Concepcion, for their compassion and kindness. To my brothers, Chevo, Jimmy, Eddie and Fernando, for their concern and assistance. To my scleroderma friends who battle this disease each day and whose uplifting spirits motivated me to complete this book.

CONTENTS

Preface

The haggard, weather-beaten face loomed before me. Who was this person staring back at me? Her hallow, blank stare revealed the pain and sadness she struggled to conceal from the world. Yet, a glimmer of light flickered in her eyes and, in that split second, I realized I was looking at my own reflection, a remnant of my former vibrant self. The reflection before me was not the familiar face I was accustomed to greeting every day. Someone played a cruel joke. If I wait a bit longer, I am sure that prankster will jump out laughing thrilled at having played this joke on me.

It has been ten years since I have grudgingly allowed this trespasser to invade my space. Would I accept her companionship? Before me is a figure of an old, feeble, frail and thin woman. Yet, I knew in my heart, I had to accept her

1

presence in my life. How could this be possible? I am 48 years old, yet I have the physique of a senior citizen. Not long ago, I recall having an athletic and youthful physique. I was an attractive and energetic woman, in the prime of her life, with an easy-going nature. I took pride in my appearance and people would guess I was years younger than my actual age. Now, people think my mom and I are sisters. Funny, how unpredictable life can be.

My once full, lustrous, shiny hair has been traded for thin, dull, brittle hair that barely grows. My beautiful, straight, white teeth are yellowish and have shifted into a crooked overbite. My mouth is smaller and, when I talk, I can not open my mouth completely, so I look as if I am talking with clenched teeth. My olive-colored, even toned skin changed almost overnight into a dark, blotchy, pockmarked complexion. My facial hair is sparse, giving my eye lashes and eye brows a barely noticeable appearance.

One day, I went into a video store to rent some videos. The store clerk behind the counter asked me, "Were you in a fire?" I was clueless to the nature of her question, so I replied, "Why, do I smell like smoke?" She said, "No, my brother looked like you only he was in a fire. He ended up committing suicide." I then realized my blotchy complexion was the reason for her comment. What could I say after hearing that remark? I felt as if the wind got knocked out of me, but I am good at masking my feelings. I do not remember what else I said to her. I handed her some bills, grabbed my videos and walked out of the store. I pretended it did not bother me. But it did.

Sometimes I would run into acquaintances who, after not having seen me in a long time, would say, "What happened to you? I remember when you looked healthy?" Or, I have an even better comment, a person once told me, "I know what you have, that's the old people's disease." Yeah, thanks I needed to hear that. I would let those words roll off my back.

Every morning, I pull out my makeup case and, with intense concentration, pencil in eyebrows and carefully outline my eyes and lips. This is a ritual I perform every day. I would not dare expose what lies beneath or leave my house looking otherwise. It is not for vanity's sake, but to avoid as many stares as possible. My once beautifully shaped, oval eyes are now smaller, round and set back into sunken eye sockets. There is no visible fat in my face so it appears drawn and taunt. My lips are so thin they remind me of two horizontal lines connected at each end. That leaves my proboscis. I have always had a large nose. Now, it is pinched and pointy, like a toucan bird's beak.

The body attached to this head has undergone its own transformation. My once straight posture is hunched and stooped, with my shoulders drawn inward. Would you believe in high school I was in a posture contest? I did not win, but, someone there told me, maybe it was my homeroom teacher, I walked straight and proud like a queen. I am sure my body language projected a confident stride. My bony arms are dark brown with emaciated muscles. I imagine birds mistaken them for tree branches. I keep them covered with long sleeves, even on extremely hot days. My lithe, graceful fingers are bent into bird claws. A lawyer I worked for once told me I had nice hands.

Now, we have the lower half of my anatomy. My legs and feet are not so bad in appearance except for limited function. I can't fully bend my knees making simple tasks, such as picking up a coin or taking a bath, impossible. The soles of my feet are very sensitive to excessive walking. Since calluses are a constant problem, giving my feet a pedicure is a challenge.

My weight dropped from a robust 145 pounds, down to 87 pounds. Can you imagine undergoing this transformation within a one-year period? The life I was accustomed to disappeared, seemingly overnight. What happened? Did I have a warning? No, I did not.

This is why I am telling my story, to give hope to others with an illness, because in spite of my bitching, I am making it. I would like to also remind people, who are healthy, to cherish their health because, with no fair warning, it can disappear. This is the story of how I developed a disease most people never heard of, it is called scleroderma.

Scleroderma is a systemic disorder of connective tissue characterized by induration and thickening of the skin, abnormalities of the blood vessels, and fibrotic degenerative changes in various body organs. There are three subtypes of localized scleroderma: localized, affecting the outer skin, generalized morphea, characterized by patches of hardened skin, and linear, characterized by large patches of thick skin merging into each other. There are three subtypes of systemic scleroderma (also known as systemic sclerosis): limited, also referred to as CREST, representing calcium deposits, Raynaud's Phenomenon, esophageal dysfunction, sclerodactyly and telangiecstatia. The next form is diffuse, where the exterior skin, internal organs and vascular system are affected. The last form is called sine, meaning "without" where the outer skin is not affected. The internal organs are affected, making this form difficult to diagnose. Each and every one of these forms of scleroderma is life altering and devastating. Systemic scleroderma is a multi-system disease and the most life threatening. This is the form I was diagnosed with.

Chapter I

The Early Years

When did the demise of my health begin? At the age of 39, I hardly recall catching a cold or being sick. I was 5'3" and weighed 145 pounds. I wanted to lose a few pounds and look trim, so I exercised and ran, three to five times a week, five miles at a stretch. I enjoyed yearly vacations with my daughters, attended family functions and social gatherings; in fact, I was the dance initiator at parties. I lived a normal and fulfilling life, lacking only in the dating scene, I guess my standards were too high.

My story begins in 1993. I was in my early thirties, confident, optimistic, always believing in overcoming obstacles. I had grown weary of fifteen years of legal secretarial work and I was ready for a career change. The drone of the printers, the monotony of office politics, rumor mill, commute and pollution became a boring routine. My life was on auto pilot and I desperately needed a challenge. I decided to try something entirely new. Coincidentally, the police department and post office were hiring. Both jobs were good opportunities with excellent benefits. I thought, "Why not apply? It couldn't hurt." I submitted applications for both jobs.

In my personal life, I was a single parent raising two daughters, Natalie, who was five, and Megan, who was three. Natalie was a ball of energy, always moving, inquisitive and fearless. Megan was the opposite, quiet, gentle and sensitive. Both were adorable, beautiful and intelligent girls. They were continuous moving entities and I enjoyed spending every moment with them. I found single parenthood as challenging as a circus act, like balancing a ball on my head, juggling and riding a unicycle, all at once. I was fortunate that my mom helped out by watching my daughters while I worked.

Natalie attended kindergarten and was having difficulty with vowels and the alphabet. I tried my best to help her, but when I arrived home at six or seven o'clock in the evening, I had very little energy left. Usually I would reheat dinner, wolf down my meal, catch up on the day's events and prepare for the next day. I realized at this important juncture, Natalie needed my help more than ever and I resolved to make time for her.

At work, an opening for a night shift secretary became

available. It was the solution to my current predicament. I thought this situation would be ideal. I would work at night, while my children slept, take them to school in the morning, snooze for a few hours, and pick them up after school. Nowhere in my imagination did I have a clue what working the night shift would be like. I was offered the position and took on a full load. No doubt my girls were worth every bit of my new schedule. With a few hours of sleep, I worked, tutored Natalie and ran the household.

On my days off, I planned activities with my children. We would go to the museum, park, zoo or beach and spend the whole day there. Some weekends we would barbeque at my sister's house and spend the night. Gradually, my energy level dwindled with the pace of my night job. One morning as I napped, I woke up to find my daughters standing before me, one holding a plate with scrambled eggs, and the other, a glass of juice. They wanted to surprise me and cooked my breakfast. I ate the crunchy eggs, burnt toast and drank the juice wholeheartedly, while they watched me, proud of their accomplishment. It was the best breakfast I ever had.

After a few months, one of Natalie's teachers approached me after school and asked, "Are you helping Natalie with her school work? I notice you pick her up from school now." I said, "Yes, I am spending more time with her." He replied, "I am amazed at how much she has improved in such a short time! She is on the honor roll and getting A's and B's." We both knew my participation made a difference. I relished the news and smiled the whole way home.

The new schedule was paying off with good results. I knew my daughter would have a better chance to compete in this world. Thinking back, sometimes parents at the grammar school thought I was a teacher. Maybe it was because I volunteered at the school and participated in the PTA and local school council. By volunteering, I could help the teachers and keep a watchful eye on my children.

After a few months, working the night shift began to take a toll on me. I developed that zombie, glass-eyed, dazed look common among graveyard shift workers, but I chose to ignore it and carry on as usual. I attended my daughters' field trips, gymnastic competitions, t-ball games, swimming classes and brownie meetings. I thought I was the invincible super mom!

Chapter II

Going Postal

I n 1994, I received a letter from the post office advising me to come in and take a written test. At the age of 35, I realized I had to find a job with good opportunities and retirement benefits. The post office was stable and fit this description. At last, when the test date arrived, I was ready. The test was not difficult and I passed with a good score. Within months, I was offered a position as a mail handler at the Bulk Mail Center ("BMC") in the Maywood branch. I accepted and could not wait to begin my new job.

I left my job with the law firm and started my new job at the post office. The first day began with orientation. All the new employees were gathered into the cafeteria. It was filled with roughly four hundred people talking and milling about. Most of the employees were minorities whose backgrounds consisted of 85% black, 13% Hispanic and 2% white. Everyone was animated with excitement. We had no idea where we were going or what we would be doing, but, the excitement was contagious. After what seemed like an eternity, supervisors holding clipboards, filed into the cafeteria. They began calling names and sorted employees into groups. We were then led to our work station.

As I walked through the BMC, I noticed its vast size and enormity. It reminded me of an airplane hangar, except it was dark and dusty with conveyor belts, loaded with sacks and boxes, moving in different directions. The loading docks had semi-trucks backed up to their assigned door, waiting to get loaded or unloaded. Postal workers were stationed high up above, near the ceiling, where they would scan sacks of mail or manually key in zip codes.

One section, called sack shakeout had workers clipping sacks of mail upside-down on a line. They would open the sacks and the back and forth shaking of the line would force the mail to fall out of the sacks. Some workstations were more sought after than others. This section was one of them.

I was assigned to the loading docks, one of the hardest jobs in the center, I found out later. The job involved extending a conveyor belt 20 to 30 feet into a truck. Since the conveyor belt did not reach the full length of the truck, workers had to lift each sack of mail, weighing 30 to 50 pounds, and drag it to the front of the truck. This was a preventive measure to keep the truck from jackknifing. Once the front of the truck was completely filled, one could run the conveyor belt nonstop dropping the sacks into the truck.

The whole setup might be hard to imagine, but it was undoubtedly, physically hard and dirty work. Every conveyor belt was assigned a zip code. Some belts had more mail and ran heavier, especially during the holidays, when crates of fruit, mailed gifts and annual catalogues came through. The loading docks had light signals, alerting supervisors and management when the conveyor belts were backed up with mail. A green light indicated the conveyor belt was clear, yellow indicated an average amount, but red meant the mail was backed up and the supervisor would come running like a hoard of bees was after him, yelling, "The mail is backed up! What is going on? You have to run the mail out!" As if we did not know and could not see for ourselves.

There were ten of us working the east dock, five men and five women. We were each assigned three to four trucks. Our supervisor gave the heaviest running conveyor belts to me and the guys, which we did not know at the time. I got along with the guys and learned they were from Gary, Indiana. Our work was strenuous and exhausting and we rested every chance we got.

After a week or so it became obvious that our supervisor was attracted to one of the female workers. He was always talking to her and the other girls. This explained why he had given her and her friends the lightest running conveyor belts. It seemed like they were standing around all the time, lollygagging, while the rest of us ran back and forth running the conveyor belts. After weeks of this nonsense, my co-workers and I began to feel resentment; and, during one of our bitching sessions, I said, "I am going to the union. You can either come with me or stay behind. But, if I go alone, I am complaining on my own behalf." I stressed we had to do this as a group to give our case credibility. Needless to say, they followed me to the union office.

Somehow, our supervisor got wind of our intentions to file a complaint. As we were walking into the union office, he was walking out. Apparently, he thought if he got there first and gave his side of the story, he would have the upper hand. The union representative heard our complaints and believed our version. The next day, our supervisor was reassigned his old job, driving a forklift.

The funny part of this episode is that our former supervisor complained about me to everyone and gave the impression that I was a large, nasty, mean and intimidating woman. When people met me and found out I was the person who got the supervisor reassigned, they all laughed at him, especially, since I am diminutive in size and not intimidating, at least not physically.

Our working conditions did not get easier for those of us working on the dock. The new supervisor watched us like a hawk and hounded us all day long. I believe some postal supervisors lean hard on their employees to guarantee their job status. Unions can only do so much to protect one's rights. The work was physically exhausting. In the winter, the docks were freezing, and in the summer, they were sweltering hot.

As soon as my probationary period ended, I put in a bid for the graveyard shift. My bid went through and I went back to working the night shift. The best part was leaving the docks and transferring to the sack shakeout section. Occasionally, I worked as a keyer and received a higher pay rate. I noticed the difference in my work environment immediately. The supervisors were nicer and the work was not as strenuous. On my way to lunch, I would glance over at the docks watching the workers running back and forth from truck to truck. It was a difficult job and my heart went out to them.

After the first two weeks, I was back to feeling like a zombie driving home in the morning and I am sure I looked like one too. One morning, I was so tired I pulled over to the side of the expressway to catch a fifteen minute snooze. It was the safest thing for me to do. This job was the most physically and mentally demanding work I ever did. I developed an admiration for postal workers because I walked in their shoes. I knew with my skills and background I could leave the post office at any time and move on to other opportunities. But that was not the case for everyone. I would bide my time until the right opportunity came along.

Chapter III

Peace and Order

My days were full and I enjoyed the time spent with my family. I gradually adjusted to my routine when, in the summer of 1994, I got a notice from the police department to come in and take a written test. I felt this was an opportunity I could not pass. On the day of the exam, I was nervous as I drove to the location mentioned in the letter. I was astounded by the endless stream of applicants making their way to the entrance. Would I stand a chance considering the competition? I sat down at my assigned desk and looked at the test laid out before me. When the signal to begin was given, I focused on each question and with intense concentration wrote down the best answers. When I completed the last question, I let out a sigh of relief. Now it was a matter of waiting.

I tried not to think about the test results, but every day, I checked the mailbox with anticipation. Finally, I received a large, yellow envelope from the police department. I thought this had to be a good sign. When I read the first line of the letter, I could not believe my eyes, I passed the exam with an above-average score. I was ecstatic at the fantastic news! Soon, thereafter, I received notices to undergo a psychological test, medical exam, physical strength and endurance test followed by a drug test. In the meantime, I continued working nights at the BMC hoping my days were numbered. The tests were given in the daytime so they did not interfere with my job. Throughout the hiring process, I forged through each test with a fierce determination to succeed. I could not believe when all the testing was completed and I had successfully passed all the requirements. I was still working at the post office when I got the official letter of acceptance from the police department. This was the best news ever! I turned in my resignation at the post office, glad to leave it behind in a distant memory. It was an experience I would never forget.

Once again, I reminded myself I could attain whatever goals I set for myself. One of my mantras is "Believe you can achieve" and I hoped to instill the same belief in my daughters. Any time they would say to me, "I can't do this," I would respond with, "Yes, you can and you will." By the same token, I was not an overly strict disciplinarian. I encouraged them to do their best and I wanted them to enjoy their childhood.

I prepared myself mentally for my first day at the academy. I knew in this line of work women were the minority and frowned upon when choosing this career. I would not let those ideas deter me from performing well in the academy.

In March of 1995, I arrived at the academy wearing my khaki uniform to begin training as a recruit. This was an exciting time for me. To have come this far was a major achievement. I persisted with my usual intensity in overcoming whatever obstacle came my way. We were tested weekly on the subjects we studied during the week. I thought physical training was the most difficult class. At the end of each physical training class, I would find myself dripping in a puddle of sweat. My favorite class was the firearms class. Even though I had never fired a weapon, I was one of the top shooters in my class. I was affectionately given the nickname "Annie Oakley". Firing a gun came naturally and I glowed over my scores.

My tenacity paid off and I completed the six month training at the academy. In our final week we were given district assignments. I was assigned to a district on the southwest part of Chicago, where I would begin my probationary period working the third watch (1600 to midnight). In September of 1995 we had our graduation ceremony where I graduated in my official blue uniform.

My life entered a new phase. I was very proud of my

achievements so far. On my first day, I arrived at the district wearing my spanking new, blue uniform and polished silver badge. The black leather gun belt I wore was stiff and buckled tightly around my waist. Each separate pocket contained mace, handcuffs, magazines and my sigsauer was secured and holstered in place. I had the proper training and was ready to utilize my equipment. Roll call began and, one by one, each name was called and answered with "Here". After roll call, the commander introduced the new recruits to their training officers.

The training officer assigned to me was an Irish female by the name of Jean. She had short, brownish-red, wispy hair and wore no makeup on her freckled face. She had a deep, raspy voice and a relaxed, yet stern, manner about her. Jean possessed a sense of humor, was amicable, and I could tell we would get along. I was glad to have her assigned as my training officer. Over the months, I learned a lot about police work from her. Whether we were pulling a car over, making an arrest, or assisting other officers, she was street-smart and a force to be reckoned with. I learned safety was the number one factor. We developed an unspoken language and, with a simple glance, knew what the next move would be. We protected each other and worked as a team.

Patrol officers and their partners spend more time together than some married people. I learned police work can be exciting, terrifying, boring and heart-pounding, all in one day. It was everything and nothing you could imagine. My adrenaline would race through my body within split seconds of getting a high risk job, and drop back to normal a short time later, throughout my shift. I understood why coppers develop an uncanny sense of humor with each other, diffusing the tension after an offender was caught and peace restored. Then we were off to the next call. No two days were ever the same. Every day before I left for work, I would put on my uniform, buckle my gun belt, look in the mirror and beam with pride. I knew I was in a position to make a difference in other people's lives and I enjoyed every minute of it.

The district I worked in had an interesting group of police officers. Everyone's personality stood out. The differences were obvious, so naturally, we gravitated to the ones we felt comfortable with. As a whole, the camaraderie was unique, unlike any other job. Everyone looked out for each other, especially on calls that posed a high risk. At the end of the day, we'd converge at the station to turn in our radios and paperwork. We'd joke around with each other as we waited to check out and we were glad to end the day safe and sound.

After I completed my probation, I was asked by Jean and her partner, Judy, to join them as the third man on their squad car. The ideal situation is to have an assigned squad car, otherwise, one would float and fill in for other officers. I accepted their offer.

In the summer of 1996, my health was not bad even though I subsisted on a regular diet of fast food, mostly fried, soda, coffee and snacks. It is hard eating healthy when you're on the run for eight hours. I gradually packed on an additional fifteen pounds, but it did not interfere with the duties of my job. I developed a thicker waist but, it did not slow me down, I could still run after the bad guys.

In the fall, I put in a bid to transfer to the night shift (0000 to 0800). Regardless of my career choice, my focus remained on spending as much time possible with my daughters. My bid went through and I began working the first watch. I wasn't familiar with the first watch officers, so I floated for a while. It was a great way to work with and meet everyone. After a month or two, I joined John and Paul on their beat car. Things were falling into place. I had the dream job with fantastic benefits. Life was grand!

Chapter IV

Hard Knock Life

The following year, in July of 1997, I began searching for a house. At the time, we were living in an apartment and I felt it was time to buy our own piece of property, where we could enjoy the freedom that comes with owning a house. A realtor showed me many homes and was excited to show me one in particular. She said it was a bargain and needed some work. I heard my favorite word "bargain". I did not fall in love with the house right away. It was a bit shabby, but with some money and a little bit of love, I could bring it back to life. So I signed on the dotted line and invested in the fixer upper.

The house was 60 years old, had an antiquated kitchen

and carpeting that bore a dirty path leading from the front doorway to the dining room. There were two small bedrooms and a tiny bathroom. I liked the original woodwork and the fact that it was not painted over. The unfinished, musty smelling basement had the typical grey cement floor and walls. An old washer and dryer, still in working condition, were left behind by the previous owner. The best part was the yard had plenty of room for a small garden and my daughters to run around and play.

Before we moved in, we cleaned and mopped the house from all the accumulated years of dust. An elderly woman had lived there and the house had been vacant for quite some time. Our lease at the apartment ended before we begin painting the interior of our new home. I thought no big deal we would manage simply by moving the furniture around.

The whole interior of the house needed a fresh coat of paint and all the carpeting had to get pulled and replaced. I began purchasing supplies when a friend mentioned she had leftover paint I could help myself to. I went to her house where she led me to a stack of various cans of paint. I grabbed a five gallon bucket of basic white paint, glad to save myself a few bucks. Unfortunately, I did not notice the warning on the label on the side of the bucket. (Later, I found out it was industrial paint and not meant for household use.) The few dollars I saved would cost me more in the end.

In early fall, I began the task of painting the interior of the house. I did not mind painting and found it therapeutic. I would get lost in my thoughts as I rolled the roller back and forth, covering the faded and dull walls, bringing new life to the house. When I finished, I noticed the fumes were very strong, so I tried to pry open the windows. Because there were many layers of paint on the window frame, I could not open the windows more than a few inches. The smell made sleeping difficult, but eventually, the fumes dissipated after several days. The carpet installers arrived later that week. Once again, there was a strong chemical odor, this time from the adhesive which we were forced to bear with until the smell to wore off. Within weeks, most of the renovation was completed. I was satisfied that my house was coming together and feeling like a home. Just in time, one month before the winter season.

Chicago's winters are bitter and cold. This winter was no different. It arrived one morning, blasting frigid northerly winds and leaving a blanket of snow in its wake. Late that evening, I grabbed a shovel and went outside to tackle the snow. When I re-entered my warm, toasty house, I looked down at my fingers, and noticed a few of them were whitish and felt numb. I thought this was strange and unusual. After a while my fingers tingled as they warmed up and the blood circulation returned. My daughters' father, Mike, stopped by, and I mentioned this weird phenomenon to him. We both chalked it up to a one time occurrence and I did not give it a second thought.

A few days later, while at work, I was getting out of my squad car and, once again, noticed the same numbing and tingling sensation. This time, I thought the explanation for this strange phenomenon was a simple matter of wearing gloves. I would be more diligent about covering my hands in the future. I still had no cause for alarm.

After a few months, the harsh winter was over and the snow was beginning to melt. A new development was taking place in my body. The strange, tingly finger sensations had progressed and now included joint pain. The excruciating pain had spread into my hands and feet. My fingers looked like swollen sausages and the bottoms of my feet burned. I popped some over-the-counter pain pills into my mouth and made a mental note to see a doctor and have some testing done.

During this time, I was feeling stressed, both physically and mentally. I was pushing myself beyond my limitations and the wear and tear was taking a toll. Even though I was concerned, I was not alarmed. I would get through this as I always did. Surely I thought, I was experiencing the early signs of arthritis and, with medication, my symptoms were treatable.

Chapter V

Genes and DNA

The next few months passed with bouts of pain and my health did not improve. I considered it a nuisance and not a major problem. In a pensive mood, I would pick my brain to try and figure the source of my medical condition. That's when memories of my maternal grandmother flashed through my mind. I remembered, when I was eight years old, going on a family road trip to Mexico, to visit my mom's family. All nine of us piled into our station wagon and prepared ourselves for the long journey. Yes, you heard right! My parents, four brothers, two older sisters, and I, cramped like sardines, sandwiched between suitcases, made the long, three-day trip to Mexico.

When we reached our destination, we had to leave our station wagon behind in the pueblo and complete the journey by foot. We walked the remaining two to three miles, lugging our bags and suitcases. Visions of my family carrying suitcases, walking through dusty clay roads, lined with endless fields of corn, leading to my grandparents' ranch, played back in my mind. It was so hot, I could barely breathe. We were tired as we meandered through the endless road. Finally, we reached our destination that ended at the top of a hill. I noticed what looked like a well to our left, something I had seen only in books, and, just beyond it, were several small huts. On the right, stood two larger dwellings with red tiled roofs, separated by the road. Small barefoot children, and loose chickens, were running around haphazardly. People, I did not know, were smiling and hugging all of us. Later, I learned they were my aunts, uncles and cousins.

The first large house on the right, surrounded by an eight foot high brick wall, had a massive door that dominated the entrance. A huge oak tree, with a tire dangling on a rope from one of its branches, towered high above to the right of the entrance. This was my great grandmother's house. The other house, across the road was not as imposing. This one belonged to my grandparents. Both homes had concrete floors with spacious, airy rooms. They were sparsely furnished with simple, wooden furniture. The windows were basic square openings with no window panes. At night, the wooden shutters were closed and locked, to keep out creatures, critters and bugs.

My great grandmother's house had a large courtyard filled with luscious plants and caged colorful birds, mostly parakeets. When I visited her home, my eyes were wide and filled with wonder. It reminded me of a castle or a mansion because there were so many rooms. I imagined my great grandmother was the queen. Her house, with its many rooms, was quiet and peaceful except for the chirping of the birds. Visiting her house was more a formal affair. After knocking on the massive door, a housekeeper would let me in and lead me to the kitchen where, my great grandmother would be relaxing and enjoying her afternoon tea. My visits were usually short and sweet because I did not know how to speak Spanish very well.

The nine of us stayed at my grandparent's house. Their house was the complete opposite of my great grandmother's. There was so much life and activity going on. My grandmother was a short, petite woman who always wore a gentle smile on her face. Her skin was porcelain white and she had pitched black hair. She wore dark clothing, such as a long black skirt with a white blouse, and, usually covered her shoulders with a black sweater or shawl. You might wonder what does any of this have to do with my health. The one physical trait that I remember was her hands, which, even though she tried to hide them, I could tell she was self-conscious about them. The fingers on both hands were bent to the side in an odd, crippled form. Even though she was in pain, she never complained. At night, while my aunts helped

27

her get undressed and prepare her bed, I could hear her attempts to hide her pain.

My grandmother gave us unrequited love and a cheerful welcome throughout our visit. All our wants and needs were immediately provided for by one of our aunts. Her house was filled with her children and grandchildren. You could hear the sounds of laughter and the drone of talking while my aunts cooked and cleaned for my grandmother. There was so much love in that ranch, it permeated the air! I had never felt that kind of love before, or since. In my eyes, my grandmother was a saint. She made sure we were each treated special.

My grandfather was just as loving. He would hug us and tell us how much he loved us. My uncles would ride horses and take the cows out to pasture each day. They also took care of the crops. In the day, I would visit my aunts' homes and watch them cook or clean. Even the boring days were fun. This was a different, simple world that I was not familiar with, and where everyone was happy. I felt like we were at a festival because of the party-like atmosphere.

As the memory faded away, I was brought back to my current predicament. Perhaps, these were the early signs of arthritis. I knew there was medication to treat arthritis, and many people are able to live productive lives. I still had not made the time to see a doctor, but it was a priority on my list. In the meantime, I increased the number of pain pills I took for pain relief.

Chapter VI

The Mystery Revealed

In April of every year, the police department holds its annual health fair, where one could have a physical checkup, or, choose from a variety of tests. I imaged this was a good place to start. I attended, had blood drawn for the arthritis test, and waited for the results. A few weeks later, I received a letter stating I had abnormal results and further testing was recommended. This confirmed what I had known all along, that I had to see a doctor.

I was always healthy for the most part and never had to see a doctor, except for routine school physicals. I approach problematic situations in an organized, matter-of-fact mode.

For every problem, there is a solution. Still not worried, I pulled out the voluminous phone book, flipped through it, and came across the words "Hospitals" and "Rheumatology". I would get to the bottom of this mystery, and nip it in the bud, once and for all. I dialed the number and made an appointment at the Rush Presbyterian Hospital.

I arrived for my appointment feeling apprehensive. The nurse asked me the usual questions and wrote my medical history on her clipboard. She led me to a small room, with pink walls, and told me the doctor would be in shortly. When the doctor came in, she asked me to describe my symptoms. I explained what had been going on the past five months. The doctor gave me a physical exam, and did something I thought unusual. She took a liquid dropper and dripped an oily substance onto my fingernail bed. She then peered through a magnifying glass observing my fingernail bed. Apparently, this confirmed whatever she believed was causing my symptoms. She said, "I believe you have scleroderma. It is an autoimmune disease that causes the collagen to overproduce and the skin to harden. Right now there is no cure. It is hard to predict how each person will be affected by this rare disease. I will print out some information for you to read, and I suggest you read as much as you can about this disease. In the meantime, I can prescribe D-penicillimine medication. There is no proof these pills work, but it can possibly slow down the symptoms." I could not understand or believe what I was hearing! What was she talking about? I never heard of this disease. Did she say no cure? Well, how bad can it be?

There must be some mistake. This condition is so uncommon that the doctor did not know what dosage to prescribe. I listened as she made a phone call to a doctor at another hospital asking for the dosage. I made a mental note of the doctor's name and decided I would go directly to that doctor.

I felt numb driving home that afternoon. The sheets of paper she printed out described the disease as a rare condition, where healthy tissue begins to attack itself, causing the skin to harden. In systemic cases, the internal organs are affected and could lead to death. Its cause is unknown and there is no cure. The life expectancy could be anywhere from 1 to 2 years in extreme cases, to 20 plus years. I could not believe it. No cure? I could die? I refused to believe it was that bad. I felt like I was given a death sentence. I was hardly ever sick. This strange disease, with a weird sounding name, sounded horrible. It is not possible. Maybe it's not so bad. Maybe she made a mistake. Thoughts of denial were racing through my mind. How do I explain this to my family and friends, when I did not even understand it?

At this point, the doctor said it was a wait and see situation. I did not want to wait and see, because I felt the disease was still in its early stage and we could probably stop this beast before it had a firm grip on me. With other diseases, isn't that the rule, early diagnosis and immediate treatment would stop the progress of a disease. Medication and close monitoring would even cure a person from their illness. Right? When I saw my mom, I repeated what the doctor told me. Like myself, my mom had never heard of this disease and did not understand what the diagnosis meant. She still believed I was suffering from overwork and fatigue. I decided I would seek another doctor's opinion. Someone who could help me beat this scleroderma. I was not going down without a fight!

Chapter VII

The Chase Begins

Time ceased to exist. My mind, no longer at peace, was in constant turmoil. There was a war headed my way with an invisible enemy. I did not know what to expect. I pushed onward with my job and home life. Hopefully, the doctor at the teaching hospital could give me a better prognosis. I made an appointment with the rheumatologist and prayed for the best outcome.

At work, I concentrated on portraying a sense of normalcy, but, my acting skills were not up to par. It was becoming difficult to hide my discomfort. One night, as my partner and I were finishing paperwork at the station, one of the officers asked me what was wrong. I was not ready to talk about my uncertain fate, so I told her I had arthritis. I could tell from the look on her face that my discomfort was obvious.

I finally went to see the rheumatologist who specialized in scleroderma. I felt I would get the answers to my questions, and, the most up-to-date medical treatment. The doctor I went to see was highly regarded in this field. Unfortunately, my experience with him did not prove to be a positive one. His waiting room was always packed, wall-to-wall, with patients. Some of them were pushing oxygen tanks, and, there was always an hour's wait. I assumed he had to be a very good doctor. Yet, I could not deny the alarm I felt at seeing such sickly patients. I did not have a good feeling about this disease.

On my first visit, he stated that D-penicillimine was the only drug used to treat scleroderma at that time. It would take at least six months before I would see any signs of improvement. Before this drug takes effect, a patient's condition could even worsen and there was no guarantee D-penicillimine would work. This did not make sense to me. Six months is a long time to wait while my health deteriorated. I had no other option except to give it a try. Mind you, I was new to the medical environment, and, being from the old school, thought the doctor knows best. I believed doctors had the ability to make a person well. My naivety would come back to haunt me.

This was a trying time for me since I was in excruciating pain. How do you advocate for yourself while you're in pain and from what? My doctor prescribed Ultram for the pain and this helped relieve the pain immediately. I finally could sleep at night. But it was a band aid. I could envision the poisonous disease, coursing through my body, attacking everything in its path. Every day brought me closer to some horrible unknown fate.

At each monthly appointment, the doctor would smile at me and ask his routine "How are you?" It was so mechanical and fake. I wanted to say "I am dying. What do you think? What are you doing for me?" But I didn't. I did not feel a sense of urgency from him or that he really cared. He was not aggressive about fighting this disease. I did not feel he was my partner in this race against time, in fending off this disease. If anything, I felt he was an observer on the sidelines. He would get paid whether I got better or not. What was his incentive? I thought there was no purpose in going to these appointments if all he did was document my deterioration. On one of those visits, I told him I was experiencing depression and could he prescribe something for it. He said he would prefer that I attend a support group instead. I was too fatigued to go anywhere and never went. Instead, I dealt silently with my depression. On another occasion, I was experiencing difficulty breathing, especially when I was laying down. I called the doctor's office and spoke with the nurse. I told her I could not breathe. She told me to turn on the hot water in the shower and breathe in the steam. I did not feel I was getting the proper attention. My breathing was not a simple matter of inhaling steam. I did not have asthma, I had scleroderma. I tried her suggestion, it did not work. I wanted to talk to the doctor, who was never available, and he did not even call me back to see how I fared.

Chapter VIII

A Spring Promise

I managed to keep working but I knew my future as a police officer was uncertain. After three or four months of my diagnosis, I told my partners and my lieutenant about my prognosis. They encouraged me to stay on as long as I could, which I did. They were very sympathetic and supportive of my situation. However, by the end of August, there was no denying the fact that I could not perform the job I worked so hard for. I had a hard time gripping objects and I did not even have the strength to twist the top off a water bottle. I reluctantly went on medical disability with the belief that my leave was temporary. I convinced myself that my health would improve and, eventually, I would return to work.

But my health continued its downward spiral. Now, I became nauseous immediately after eating. The D-penicillimine medication didn't help because it had an awful sulfuric taste and exacerbated the nausea. I threw up the medication prescribed for scleroderma and the meal I had just consumed. Within five months, I lost twenty-five pounds. I was losing weight at an alarming rate. I felt at this pace, death was eminent.

Eventually, I began telling my family and friends of my pending condition, but it was difficult to talk without crying. I could not utter a complete sentence without breaking down. I cried more for my children, than I did for myself. It was not fair. What would become of my daughters without me, their protector, advocate and provider? No one would or could take my place. The fight was not over. Damn that fricking scleroderma. I became so angry! I would not let some ridiculous disease defeat me. I don't usually swear, but this situation demanded a good swearing session. I was mad, sad, angry, scared, you name it, I felt it!

One day, while on the phone with my sister, Blanca, we were discussing my situation and I asked her, "Do you think miracles still happen?" She said "I don't see why not." I responded, "Because I could sure use one right now." I am not religious, by typical standards, but I do believe in a Supreme Being. I began to pray every day, read the Bible and had midnight conversations with God, even if they were one-sided. An unusual occurrence kept happening to me during this traumatic time. I noticed on three separate occasions, and using different Bibles, every time I flipped the book open, it would open to Psalm 18. The first time I read that psalm it gave me relief and hope. I felt it was very appropriate for my situation. It was even mentioned in the sermon I attended at my friend's church.

EXCERPTS FROM PSALM 18

2   The Lord is my rock, and my fortress, and my deliverer; my God, my strength, in whom I will trust...

6   In my distress I called upon the Lord, and cried unto my God; he heard my voice out of his temple, and my cry came before him, even into his ears.

7   Then the earth shook and trembled; the foundations also of the hills moved and were shaken, because he was wroth.

17   He delivered me from my strong enemy, from them which hated me; for they were too strong for me.

I would read this psalm many times over.

My sister, Connie, a wiz at surfing the internet, searched the internet for information and available treatments for scleroderma. On a regular basis, she sent me thick packets of information, followed with phone calls, to discuss possible treatments. Connie was relentless in her quest to help me. She even came with me to one of my doctor appointments, armed with questions.

One treatment, based on an antibiotic protocol, caught our attention immediately. People, who had scleroderma, gave testimonials on how they were cured with this protocol. Their stories were recounted in a book called, "Scleroderma, The Proven Therapy That Can Save Your Life", written by Henry Scammell. In the book, Dr. Thomas McPherson Brown is described as a physician who introduced the theory that arthritis is caused by bacteria. His method of treatment consisted of daily dosages of minocycline or tetracycline, and weekly intravenous infusions of clindamycin. He utilized this regimen to treat his patients affected with scleroderma and many claimed they experienced complete reversal of the disease. Although Dr. Brown is no longer alive, doctors who studied his teachings continue to practice the antibiotic protocol to treat scleroderma. The medical community considered Dr. Brown's treatment unconventional and it was not accepted as a credible method of treating scleroderma.

I went to the library to check out the book. I could not wait to get home to start reading the testimonials of people claiming they were cured from scleroderma. I cried as I read their stories. I thought I want to get cured also. Then I came across the name of a doctor who studied under Dr. Brown. His office was located in Schaumburg, Illinois, an hour's drive from my house. I was thrilled at the prospect of getting completely cured or at least improving my condition somehow. Since my current treatment was not working, I knew it was time to switch doctors. I immediately made an appointment to meet with this doctor. The chase was on to find the cure.

By this time, the effects from scleroderma had progressed to the point where my fingers were swollen and beginning to curl. I could not make a fist or fully straighten my fingers. I underwent physical therapy to stretch my fingers and legs. I was so fatigued in the morning that it took all my energy to shower and get dressed. By pure chance, I discovered I was losing my flexibility. One day while taking a bath, I found it difficult to bend my knees to stand up. I had to flip over to my side to push myself up. It scared me when I realized my bubble bath days were over, for now. My skin color had darkened a few shades and people commented on my nice tan.

My daughters, in their pre-teen years, were aware of my unstable health. They were confused after witnessing my dramatic, physical changes. I reassured them that once I found the proper medication, my health would rebound and I would get better. I wanted to believe my own words and I maintained a brave front. I resolved after seeing this new doctor, I would get cured just like all those people in the book. It had to work and I believed it would.

It was early fall. The leaves were beginning to dry out and change to beautiful colors. On my first visit with this doctor, I came away with a good impression. He appeared sincere and very optimistic about my prognosis. He was confident that I would heal and said that by springtime I would be running. His enthusiasm was contagious and convincing. At last, I found a doctor with an aggressive attitude.

At my appointment, the doctor described his methods to treat scleroderma, which was different from traditional medicine. He was adamant in my strict adherence to his regimen. Otherwise, he stated the treatment would not work. I was given pamphlets to take home and read. I learned new methods of shopping for groceries and preparing my meals. I agreed to no longer consume sugar, flour, dairy products (except for whole butter), canned and prepackaged products, soda, processed juice or water from the faucet. Instead of red meat or pork, organic salmon and chicken were recommended. The results from my blood tests showed vitamin and mineral deficiencies. These low levels were corrected with appropriate vitamin and mineral supplements. It all sounded great and made sense to address the nutritional side of healing.

As a sign of good faith, I signed an agreement to make a life style change and commit to this program. I was given a prescription for minocycline and that very same day received a clindamycin intravenous infusion. My weight at this point was 112 pounds. Now my total weight loss was thirty three pounds. I absolutely believed I could get better and, with time, my weight would increase.

I was recharged with optimism upon my return from my appointment. I immediately went to the health food store to purchase some of the items on the list. I had never shopped at a health food store and noticed the products were expensive. I would find a way to rearrange my budget to come up with the money. It was worth a try. I was going to make this work, dammit. If I could conquer this disease and put on weight, then my life would return to normal and I would have my job back!

I explained the new diet to Natalie and Megan. They weren't exactly thrilled, but knowing it would help me get better, agreed to go along with it. Every day my mom mixed the blueberry goat milk shakes in the blender. It actually tasted pretty good. Also, as agreed, we drank purified water. Our new life style change was difficult at first, but gradually we grew accustomed to eating organic food. I'll admit giving up snacks like potato chips, cookies, donuts, cake and soda pop was hard for all of us.

After a few months, I noticed a slight change. I felt better but there were no other improvements. All my symptoms remained the same and the weight loss continued to be a problem. I learned through my research that malabsorption is a common problem in scleroderma. If the digestive system is affected, the body will not absorb nutrients or medication. This explained why I could not gain weight or why medications would not alter my condition. Every time I weighed in at the doctor's office, the numbers kept dropping. I expected the doctor to have an explanation but he said he didn't know why my weight kept dropping. I was now down to 102 pounds. This was alarming to me. I asked the doctor what was the improvement rate for his patients. He said it was 100%. I was reassured to hold on a little longer. I still held on to the belief that my health would turn around. I waited.

Spring came and went. I was not running, skipping or jumping as I imagined, and my health did not improve as I expected. My weight spiraled down to a shocking 85 pounds and we needed to reverse the weight loss. My doctor referred me to a gastroenterologist. The specialist did not have any answers or suggestions that we had not already tried. His only recommendation was that if my weight dropped to 80 pounds, I should be fitted with a food pump. He warned that my condition would most likely worsen if we got to that point. Now I was beyond worried. I had waited too long for this treatment to kick in. My doctor could not explain why my body was not responding to the regimen, even though I followed his protocol faithfully. It was a life or death situation. I desperately needed to put on weight to save my life! While on the holistic diet, fattening foods were excluded. I came to the realization, in order to save my life I had to revert to eating all the fattening foods previously banned. I gorged myself on a feast of all the unhealthy foods you can imagine. Or, at least I tried to. It was great! I never thought I would hear those words out of my mouth. Imagine that!

The antibiotic treatment and holistic regimen did not work for me. I understand the antibiotic protocol treatment has benefited other people suffering with scleroderma but, in my case, it was time to switch doctors and pursue the chase for another treatment.

My Dad and I at my niece, Kristine's 15th Catillian.

I always love a good barbeque!

Megan and Natalie, ages 3 and 5.

My friend, Joyce, and I on Graduation Day.

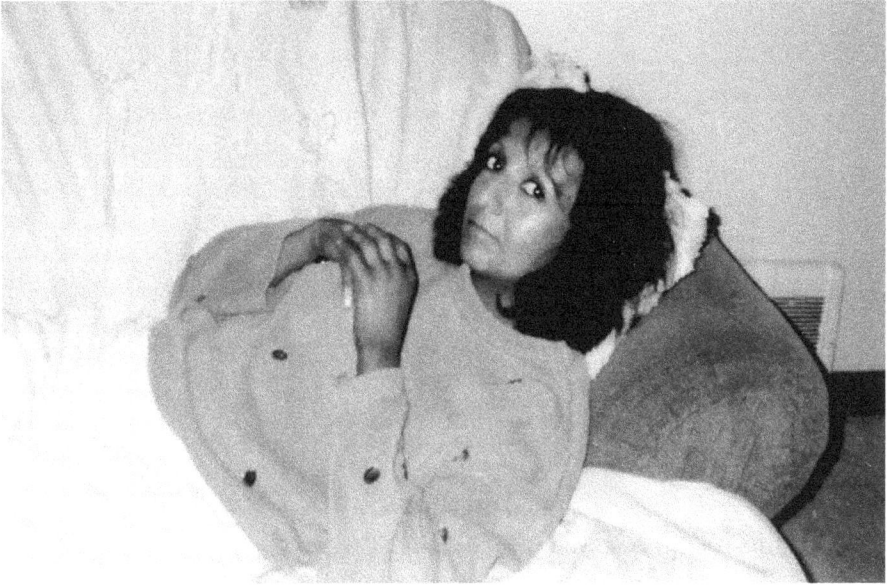

I am starting to feel like a couch potato.

Here I am enjoying the sounds of CPD bagpipers.

How do you like my brim and wheels?

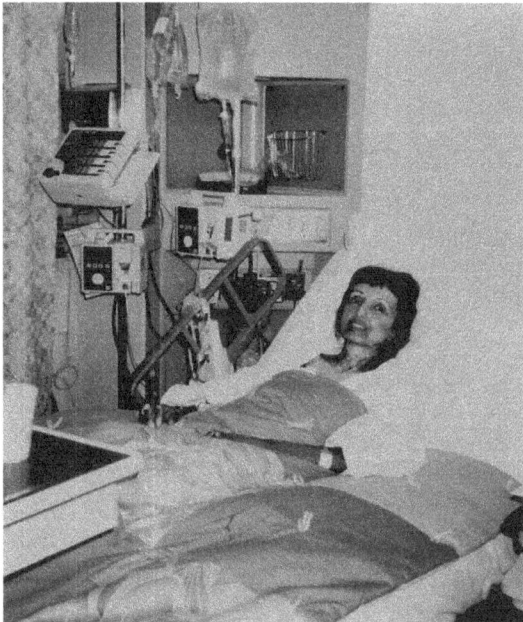

My second birthday, June 12, 2000!

Here I am sporting a cue ball coif with Boo Boo Bear.

I wonder what the chefs are cooking.

My Seattle friends, Melissa and Karen.

Mom and I, one year after transplant.

My 47th Birthday with my brothers, Eddie and Jimmy.

Natalie and Megan, all grown.

Chapter IX

Return To Traditional

Once again, attaining my dream of restoring my health eluded me. I had exhausted my funds and invested time with minor results. My body had stiffened and I ached all over. Every part of my body was affected. I could not bend my knees or stretch my arms over my head. I was extremely fatigued all the time. Taking a shower and getting dressed to go out was exhaustive. I was drained of energy before I even left the house. I could not brush my teeth with regular toothpaste because it burned my gums. At night, I would wake up intermittently from the pain. Would I dare to hope again? I cried and prayed for a miracle. It was a very lonely time for me.

No one understood what I was going through. I lay in bed all day, except when I made a run for the bathroom. If my mom hadn't stopped by to check on me, I would not have prepared myself a meal. My daughters managed their own care, doing laundry and making simple meals for themselves. When the weather warmed up, I could hear the sounds of their footsteps running in and out of the house. I was glad they were enjoying the sunshine and companionship of their friends. I wished I could play an active role in their life.

It was now late summer of 1999, and I returned to consuming regular food. I ate whatever I thought contained the highest fat content. I could not die! It was not my time to leave this world. I would do whatever was necessary to live. So I indulged in bread, cake, donuts, cookies, pancakes and lots of dairy products. I tried to eat as much as possible and resisted the urge to vomit.

I absorbed bible passages to nourish my soul and to give me strength to make it through each day. I asked God to help me in my most desperate time. I never gave up. I had to find a cure! God was always there for me in the past and I knew He would not desert me. It is funny how our Supreme Father reaches out to us. He lets us know He's here for us. It was during this time, that I was thinking of a will and potential guardians for my children. I did not know what to expect any more.

I reached deep down inside of myself for the power to continue searching for another doctor. I resolved to revisit the more popularly practiced traditional medicine. Occasionally, I spoke with other people afflicted with scleroderma and one doctor's name came up a few times. I was told he was very good. He practiced at a university nearby and I made an appointment to see him right away.

Meanwhile, God answered my prayers and my weight began to slowly creep back. Each pound was a milestone and a step toward life. A major factor in getting through the stressful periods was keeping a positive state of mind and having a lot of faith.

On my first appointment with the new doctor, my weight had reached 90 pounds. I felt a good connection with this doctor. He was a rheumatologist, very knowledgeable and had many years of experience treating scleroderma patients. I was struck by his sincerity and compassion. He said methotrexate would have alleviated the initial swelling, but in my present state, it was no longer necessary. He performed a skin score test, where he randomly pinched different areas of my skin to measure tightness. All the numbers were tallied to reach a skin score. The highest total indicated extreme skin tightening, whereas the lowest total would indicate a lesser degree. This was the first time I was tested in this manner. My skin score was a 25 which is considered high.

I mentioned to the doctor about an experimental procedure called a stem cell transplant. I asked him for his opinion and whether he thought I should consider that option. He said it was very risky and should be utilized as a last resort. Instead, he suggested I consider participating in one of the clinical studies at the university. If, at the end of the study, the experimental drug did not improve my condition, we should then consider the stem cell transplant. We ended my appointment where I agreed to contact one of the study coordinators. I was selected to participate in a study where I would give myself daily injections of a drug called eternacept. It was not too bad because the needle was tiny and felt like a mosquito bite. The hypothesis behind this study was that the skin would soften after a period of time.

Chapter X

Singing the Blues

My medical leave from the police department ended, and one day I received a letter stating that if I could not report to active duty, or another position within the department, I would have to turn in my resignation. This meant returning my identification card, badge and hat shield. In order to keep my job, I would have to pass a firearm's test. I knew this was impossible. I opened my closet door and looked at my uniform still hanging where I left it. As crazy as it sounds, I thought perhaps I could pass the firearm's test. So I took the uniform down and began to dress myself. First, I put on the shirt and then the pants. I did not know if I should bust out laughing or sit down and cry. In my clouded state of mind, I believed I could wear the uniform, take the test, and no one would notice my skeletal, debilitated appearance. It is amazing how the human mind works when we are faced with a desperate decision. I took off the uniform, put it back on the hanger, and hung it in the closet. I resigned myself to the fact that my police career was over.

The day I had been dreading came when I made the trip downtown to police headquarters. I was as thin as a rail and got plenty of stares from some officers as I walked into the lobby. I am sure many thought I was anything but a police officer. I made my way to the elevator and pressed the button for the administrative floor. I was emotionally devastated. I looked down at the silver, shiny badge I held in my hand, and ran my finger tips over the Indian figure one last time. On many occasions, I had scrutinized the details in the badge, appreciating its design.

I proceeded to walk to the area where a sergeant was sitting at his desk and stated my business. He keyed my name into the computer and peered at me over his reading glasses. Taking in my appearance, he said, "Isn't there a desk job you could apply for?" I said, "I would have to pass a firearm's test and in my present condition, that would be impossible." He responded, "That's too bad." I could tell he felt sympathy for me but officers don't say more than they have to. I handed over the shiny, silver badge with the Indian figure and the hat shield that I so proudly wore, and quietly walked out of that office with tears streaming down my face. I would never be a police officer again. I had to close the book on that chapter. The exit interview was informal and anticlimactic compared to the swearing-in ceremony. What a sad turn of events.

Besides my health, my next biggest worry was my means of income. I was the sole provider of my family and now it was impossible for me to hold down a job. Thankfully, the police family is known for helping each other. The officers at my district got together and held a benefit for me. The local fraternity of police also holds benefits for their disabled officers and they also helped me. Not everyone is so fortunate. I was truly blessed. Without their assistance, I don't know what I would have done. In the meantime, I applied for social security benefits. Through God's grace, patience and prayers from family and friends, I managed to pull through this difficult time.

Chapter XI

Renewed Faith

The days came and went. Weekends were like every other day. I began to dislike holidays. At Christmastime, I could not put up the bright and colorful lights, nor could I shop for gifts and bake dozens of cookies. My brother, Jimmy, came over one day and put my tree up for me. I gave money to a friend to buy presents for my daughters. We managed to get through that first Christmas. I always tried my best to keep a positive state of mind in front of my daughters.

I felt like a prisoner in a body that would not listen to my commands, in a home I could not enjoy. I may as well have had bars on my windows. I was an observer watching the healthy world go on without me. I did not have the energy to shop, clean, cook or bake like moms usually do. I mostly cried when I was alone. The first two years of my sickness were the hardest. I went through many psychological changes. My mom was the beacon in my life. She picked up and carried on for me when I could not. She was determined not to leave me by the wayside. She was definitely an enormous source of strength for me. My mom knew my daughters needed me and I had to get better.

In the beginning of my failing health, my daughters were confused and worried. I reassured them with the right treatment I would get better. Over time they also accepted the belief that eventually my health would return. They continued to do well in school and get good grades. They had plenty of activities to keep themselves busy. I was not able to participate in or attend school functions like I did before, but I did meet with their teachers on report card day. One thing I was adamant about and that was my appearance. I always made an effort to put on makeup and dress neatly whenever I went out in public.

My battle with scleroderma continued. This disease is relentless and unpredictable. But my visits with the doctor at the university were always positive. I looked forward to my appointments. The doctors and nurses never gave me a false sense of hope and were willing to try whatever they thought would help me. They were kind and considerate, doing their best to alleviate the pain and discomfort caused by scleroderma. I never felt like my doctor was rushing through my appointment and his responses to my calls were returned on the very same day, which I learned is not the case for all doctors. I considered myself fortunate.

After completing the clinical study, with minimal improvement, it was time for me to consider the stem cell transplant ("SCT") as a possibility. In 1999, SCTs were considered experimental treatment for scleroderma and other illnesses. It was difficult to find a medical facility conducting a stem cell transplant study for scleroderma. In my research, I found a hospital in Connecticut conducting a clinical study. One of the requirements for transplant consideration was a diagnosis of scleroderma for not more than two years and a referral from a rheumatologist.

In order to be considered a candidate, I needed copies of medical records from prior doctor visits and a confirmed diagnosis. I went to see the first doctor who treated me and explained my desire to have the SCT at the Connecticut hospital. He suggested if I wanted the best transplant facility, I should consider the Fred Hutchinson Cancer Research Center in Seattle, Washington. This center is world renown for its extensive experience in bone marrow and stem cell transplants. I could sense his disapproval in my constant search for doctors and treatments. He confirmed this when he said, "You have to make up your mind who you want for your doctor. If you decide you want me to treat you, you must let me know." Well, that took me off guard. I replied, "Okay, I will let you know," even though I had no intent or plan to return to a previous doctor. It was important to get my medical records, even if it meant getting chastised by this doctor.

Chapter XII

City of Angels

One day, while flipping through the pages of The Ladies Home Journal, I was surprised to come across an article about a young woman from Seattle, Washington with scleroderma. Her name was Kirstin Wallin and the article described her participation in the Seattle SCT study. This woman's story touched me because her health improved tremendously from the transplant. She regained her energy and mobility enough to return to college and move into her own apartment. A fire was lit under my feet to get moving and this time it was not a scleroderma symptom.

On another occasion, a friend called me and told me to turn on the television. There was a doctor on a news program talking about the stem cell transplant procedure. His name was Dr. Daniel Furst from Seattle, Washington and he was the same doctor who treated Kirstin Wallin. There was the solution right before my eyes and plain as day. Could I be so lucky? This could be the answer. Hopefully, I would be a good candidate for this transplant.

In early July of 1999, I contacted Dr. Furst's office and spoke with his nurse, Gretchen Hensdorf. I explained my situation and desire to be considered a candidate for the SCT. She told me to send them a synopsis describing my condition. I would need a diagnosis of systemic scleroderma (meaning internal and external involvement) from a rheumatologist, have an age of 45 or less, tried other treatments, have a 50% risk of mortality and/or severe scleroderma for two years or less. I definitely fulfilled those requirements. She told me to fax my medical records to them. I was thrilled and nervous at the prospect of being chosen for this study. I could not believe I was speaking to Dr. Furst's nurse. I may as well have been speaking to a movie star. What if she did not call me back? Or, even worse, what if they did not consider me a good candidate? I asked the nurse if she would promise to call me back. I was afraid my paperwork would get lost in a mountain of medical files. She assured me that she would see to it that Dr. Furst received my synopsis and medical records. I could not believe my luck. I found an angel who would help me!

Within a week, and true to her word, Gretchen called

me back with some good news. She said so far I met all the requirements and could be a potential candidate for the SCT. At last, I had a chance to regain my health and get my old life back. The next step was for me to come up to Seattle and meet Dr. Furst for an examination.

It was late fall when I boarded a plane bound for Seattle, Washington. My sister, Blanca, accompanied me on that first trip. The skies were grey and the weather was rainy and gloomy. In no way did the weather reflect my mood. I could have been blown in by a hurricane for all I cared, I was exhilarated. We were greeted at the airport by Seattle volunteers who drove us to the hotel where we had reservations. I was surprised at this unexpected welcome and later found out the Fred Hutchinson Cancer Research Center coordinates the volunteer program. It was cold that night and the rusty old heater in our room clanked and banged out very little heat. I shivered under my blanket and eventually fell asleep.

The next morning we woke up early, showered and dressed. We sipped the complimentary, hot, steamy coffee while waiting for the ancient elevator to arrive at our floor. Finally, the doors squeaked open and we went down to the lobby. We did not have to walk far or take a cab because the hospital was across the street from the hotel.

We arrived on time for my appointment. I gave the receptionist my name and waited. A few minutes later, a woman walked up and introduced herself as Gretchen. She had a soothing, calm voice and a warm smile to match the sparkle in her eyes. We followed her back to the doctor's office where she put us at ease right away. In the examination room she took my vitals and had me fill out some forms. I had gained a few more pounds and my weight was now at 95 pounds. After completing the forms and taking my vitals, the door opened, and in walked Dr. Furst. He had salt and pepper wavy hair, wire-framed glasses and also greeted us with a smile. We shook hands as he introduced himself and I appreciated his relaxed and friendly demeanor. We asked the doctor if we could tape-record our visit and he agreed. He said, "Absolutely. That's a very good idea." He began the interview by explaining the SCT agenda and outlined the sequence of events; the first was a physical examination. He was thorough and answered my questions about scleroderma and the SCT. I was impressed with his extensive knowledge of scleroderma and believed I had found the right place.

Dr. Furst explained there were two types of stem cell transplants available for the study. The first type was allogenic where the stem cells come from a compatible donor, preferably a relative. The second type was autologous where the patient's own stem cells are used in the transplant. He explained that the preparation for the SCT involved numerous tests to ensure the candidate's major organs can sustain the SCT procedure.

The next step involves the collection of stem cells from the blood using a procedure called apheresis. Before the stem cells are collected or harvested, the patient is given a mobilizing dose of chemotherapy to increase the numbers of stem cells. After the stem cells are collected, they are frozen and stored in liquid nitrogen or cryopreserved. The patient is then given high dose chemotherapy combined with partial radiation to suppress and even partially eliminate the immune system. After a few days, the purified stem cells are re-infused into the patient regenerating the immune system. The red and white blood cells begin reproducing and the blood counts begin to rise. During this dangerous period, the patient is carefully monitored for any signs of potentially dangerous side affects or infection.

Dr. Furst pointed out there were potential risks that could result from the transplant such as liver, kidney, cardiac, renal and pulmonary toxicities, skin cancer, sterility, alopecia, future malignancies and even death. He explained throughout the transplant process, I would have to reside in Seattle for a total of three months. It would also be necessary to bring a caregiver to assist me throughout my recovery. I told him I was in full agreement with the terms presented to me. I knew in my heart it was either the stem cell transplant or death. The last issue was the cost of the transplant. The allogenic procedure was more costly because it involves finding a matching donor and graft versus host disease is a major concern. After comparing the two choices, I chose the autologous SCT.

I returned home elated and renewed with hope. I immediately focused on connecting the hospital's financial department with my insurance company. In the meantime, I had to plan one more trip to Seattle to meet with the SCT medical team. They had to give their final approval before a determination was made to accept my participation in the study.

This time my sister, Connie, accompanied me on my second trip to Seattle on January 11, 2000. I was extremely fatigued from the months of preparation but we managed to get around the city as my sister pushed me in a wheel chair. I met with the members of the transplant team. They reviewed the SCT procedure in detail with me and made sure I understood the risks involved. I confirmed that I was fully aware of the potential risks and agreed to undergo the transplant.

I received the official acceptance into the study within a week. I called my family and friends with the good news. The next issue I had to contend with was finding someone to look after my two daughters while I was in Seattle. They were still in school and I would not be able to bring them and focus on my recuperation.

One late afternoon, while picking up my daughters from school, I ran into a friend named Donna Brennan, whose daughters are friends with my girls and in the same grade. I confided to her about my plans to travel to Seattle and undergo the SCT. My predicament was finding someone to watch over my daughters. She surprised me by offering to have my daughters stay with her for the duration of the school year, which would be for two months. I have known Donna for nine years. She is charismatic, friendly and a wonderful mother to her children. Her two daughters, Jaime and Becky, are the same ages as my girls, attend the same school and hang out together. I was so relieved because I knew Donna would provide a stable home and care for Natalie and Megan as if they were her own. That made a huge difference to me.

The obstacles before me were stacked like lined up dominoes, and with a solution to each problem, the dominoes were beginning to fall. The next dilemma was finding a caregiver to accompany me to Seattle. Most of the people I asked had job commitments and family obligations. Each time I dialed the phone to ask someone to accompany me, I held my breath. I kept getting apologetic refusals but I did not give up. I would leave it in God's hands. I kept my mind focused on other details, such as closing down my house, finding temporary housing in Seattle and working out the loose ends with my insurance company.

The transplant coordinator sent me a packet of information to assist me in my search for housing in Seattle. One of the apartments offered extra amenities not mentioned in the other apartments. It was an apartment complex called the Pete Gross House dedicated to the needs of cancer patients. This building was constructed specifically for cancer patients, to provide a comfortable home setting, while undergoing treatment. The Pete Gross House also provided a shuttle to transport patients and their families to and from the hospital, clinic and grocery store. I decided this would be the best choice for my temporary residence once the final arrangements were completed.

I knew God's hand was at work because one day I

received a call from a longtime friend, Patty. I have known Patty since my childhood days when she lived across the street. I remembered her being outgoing and someone who was fun to hang out with. She explained how she ran into a family member who told her of my impending health. She was sympathetic and offered to help me in whatever way she could. I mentioned the difficulty I had in finding a caregiver to come with me to Seattle. She assured me she would see what she could do, but I didn't give it any further thought.

In March of 2000 all the pieces were falling into place. All the necessary approvals and authorizations for the SCT had been received. The last surprise I received was a call from Patty. She talked to her husband and together they agreed she could accompany me to Seattle for at least one month. Someone else would have to take over the last two months. That would work. There was one more person I had not called who could help me out. I would make the call when the time came.

Meanwhile, Donna was making preparations to take in my daughters. I signed a document giving her temporary guardianship of my daughters. It was truly a miracle! I sent a deposit to the Pete Gross House for a one bedroom apartment and called my utility companies to turn off the gas and electricity. I made the travel arrangements and on April 5, 2000, my friend Patty and I boarded a plane for Seattle, Washington.

Chapter XIII

Pre-Transplant

I will admit the first two times I visited Seattle I did not pay attention to the scenery. My mind was preoccupied with other concerns. Now, I would have plenty of time to observe everything. On the plane the stewardesses were friendly and when they heard about our mission, gave us a bottle of champagne to celebrate after my transplant. They even brought us cookies from the first class section. Those cookies were delicious!

It was late in the evening when our plane landed. The Fred Hutchinson transplant coordinators had arranged for volunteers to meet us at the airport. It is a great feeling having people you don't know welcome you at the airport.

They introduced themselves and loaded our luggage into their van. We learned the driver's name was Frank and he enjoyed volunteering and helping people. We made small talk on the drive to the Pete Gross House. The sun had gone down and the interiors of homes and buildings were lit. A short while later we arrived at the Pete Gross House. We met with the building manager who had been expecting us. We thanked the volunteers and said our goodbyes. I filled out all the paperwork the building manager had prepared in anticipation of our arrival and, with keys in hand, made our way to the apartment.

Our apartment was cheerful, small and cozy. The walls were painted a pale forest green with white trim accents, matching the colors of the loveseat and sofa. The kitchen smelled like it had been scrubbed clean. The walls, cabinets and appliances were stark white. My eyes caught sight of something underneath the counter. Could it be? Yes, it was a dishwasher! Thank goodness. Everything I needed for the apartment was provided, washer, dryer, pots, pans, dishes, silverware, towels, linens and small appliances. It was not necessary for me to go out and buy anything. There was even an iron, ironing board and vacuum cleaner. The manager gave me an inventory sheet listing all the items so they could be accounted for at the end of my lease.

The next morning, Patty and I woke up bright and early. I noticed a bulletin board posted by the elevator listing various activities for the tenants. On the main floor, tenants could borrow from an assortment of videos, books, magazines and puzzles. After a quick breakfast, we set out to explore Seattle. I noticed the city was built on rolling hills. Many streets were lined with trees, shrubs and plants. To the east, a huge body of water flowed in from the Pacific Ocean, called the Puget Sound, and slightly to the north was Lake Washington. The city emanated an ultra-liberal, multicultural, alternative, rock and roll crowd. Executives in suits were intermixed with medical professionals wearing white coats. It is a great combination of different lifestyles coexisting in one city.

We took the Pete Gross House shuttle to the Swedish Hospital, located at 600 Broadway, and later to the Fred Hutchinson Cancer Research Center. We familiarized ourselves with the route and picked up my schedule of tests. As I scanned over the sheet, I noted an extensive array of tests that filled up the next two weeks. On the way back to the apartment, our driver showed us the location of the grocery store and explained how he dropped people off on the way to and from the hospital or clinic. The whole system was completely organized from the minor particulars to the major details.

Patty and I returned from my first appointment and we finished unpacking. We settled into our apartment and since I was tired from the day's events, declined her offer to go out and continue exploring the city. Meanwhile, I studied the schedule of tests required before the transplant. They included, but were not limited to, blood work, EKG, endoscopy, bronchoscope, pulmonary function test, skin biopsy, bone marrow aspiration, echocardiogram, CT scan, urine sample and x-rays, to name a few.

When Patty returned from exploring the city, she described the different boutiques and stores she encountered. We ate dinner and called it a day. As I was getting ready to turn in, as usual, my skin became unbearably itchy. It felt like a bad case of poison ivy. Patty helped put cream on my back but I still could not resist the urge to scratch.

Patty made friends easily and maneuvered through the city as if she'd lived there her whole life. I, on the other hand, spent most of my time at the apartment because I was too tired to accompany her. I had just enough energy to get to the appointments and back to the apartment. Time went by somewhat quickly but I missed my daughters and wondered what they were doing. I am sure Patty missed her family as well. She also had two daughters in grammar school and a house full of pets.

Before Patty was scheduled to return to Chicago, I made that one phone call to the one person who I thought I could count on to take over as caregiver. I called my father who lives in Arizona. I asked him if he could stay with me for the remaining two months or even just one month. He talked it over with his wife and got back on the phone. He agreed and said yes. I felt blessed and thought this would give us a chance to spend time together, which we hadn't done since I was a teenager. I was sad to see Patty leave and appreciated everything she had done for me. I knew her family back home could not wait for her to return.

My dad arrived the following week. I was so ecstatic to see him! He has a large physique and always reminded me of a huge teddy bear. He is 6 foot tall and built like a football player. When I hug him, my arms barely go around him and my hands don't reach each other. He unpacked his things and I gave him a tour of the building. He came with me to my next appointment and the nurses loved him. They signed him up for the caregiver classes where he learned techniques for changing a dressing, sterilization, applying a fresh dressing and cleaning and flushing a double-line Hickman catheter.

On May 5, 2000, I had an appointment to have the double line catheter implanted into my upper chest. The purpose of the catheter is to provide easy access for blood draws and administration of drugs. The procedure itself was not painful due to the strong pain medication I was given. I maintained a positive state of mind because I knew it would help me get through each procedure. I imagined each stage was one step closer to restoring my health. I even made a mental list of all the things I would do when I got better.

One day, my nephew Santos, stationed nearby at the naval base in Washington, came over for dinner. He did not know his grandpa, my dad, could cook and was impressed with his cooking. My dad's fish stew is out of this world. Afterward, we went to the aquarium and did some sightseeing. The following week, my brother Eddie, flew in from Chicago. We went to the Space Needle and admired the magnificent view of the city as the sun was setting over the horizon. The next day, we went to the zoo and to the popular Hiram

Chittenden Locks. When the boats leave Salmon Bay (which has fresh water), the locks are lowered and closed before releasing the boats to sea water. This process is reversed when the boats return. Visitors can also observe the salmon swimming through a glass observatory on the lower level of the pier. It is a fantastic sight to witness. My dad and I enjoyed getting out and welcomed our visits with my brother and nephew.

On Memorial Day, my dad and I received complimentary tickets to a baseball game. Would you believe the Seattle Mariner's were playing the Chicago White Sox, my home team? Naturally, Seattle won the game. We had a great time and enjoyed the best seats in the ballpark, the suite section. Thanks to a generous donation to the patients of the Fred Hutchinson Cancer Research Center, we were able to enjoy an activity we normally could not afford. The center made sure the patients had activities to stave off boredom. There were tickets for boat rides, museums and even a chance to see an opera!

Although our days were busy, I could tell my dad was becoming homesick. He missed his wife and church members, yet never complained. He would go for daily walks or take the bus to the marketplace. I was grateful for all his help and companionship.

Chapter XIV

Medical Miracle

By May 19th, the baseline work was completed and preparation for the SCT could begin. I was given bags of TPN fluid (a nutritional supplement and dehydration preventive) that had to be administered intravenously every night. The only problem I encountered was waking up in the middle of the night and running with the IV pole to the bathroom.

Three days later, the first stage of the SCT began with the removal of my stem cells. This procedure is called mobilization, where cytoxan is injected into my blood stream accelerating the production of stem cells. After a sufficient amount of stem cells were mobilized, they are intravenously collected into a machine where they undergo a procedure, called apheresis, reducing the stem cells to its earliest form. The stem cells in its purist form contain no disease or disorder and resemble regular blood. They are then cryopreserved in liquid nitrogen for future use in transplantation. Only two collections were required and taken over a two day period. The procedure reminded me of the days I used to donate blood. I stretched out on a comfortable recliner and watched television during the whole process.

The next phase is called the conditioning stage. My immune system was erased using radiation and chemotherapy. Before the radiation could commence, I was measured for shields to protect my lungs during the radiation sessions. The idea is similar to when a person is x-rayed during a dental or medical procedure, and a material made with lead is draped over the patient's extremities to protect and minimize exposure. The SCT with radiation and chemotherapy is the same procedure that's been used to treat cancer patients.

On June 5th, I was admitted to the Swedish Hospital and given a tour of the floor. My new home was a corner room with a magnificent view (on a clear day) of Mt. Rainier. I could see portions of the downtown area with the water glistening off Puget Sound. My room was brilliant white and everything spotlessly cleaned. I was introduced to the nurses on my floor, put my few belongings in the closet and prepared myself for the long haul. I was handed a sheet of procedures and rules, the most important was cleanliness. Everyone, doctors, nurses and visitors, entering or leaving the room were required to wash their hands, including myself, no exception.

My first day as an in-patient began with a series of tests in preparation for the SCT. The first was a skin allergy test for a drug called ATG. The first dosage of ATG was given to me on June 7th. I developed a slight headache and experienced flulike symptoms. By the next day I was back to feeling normal. Throughout the week, the nurses checked my vitals every hour around the clock. At night, they would wake me up at least twice, and I am not used to waking up in the middle of the night. I am a light sleeper so the sounds of the machines beeping and clicking, or the muffled talking coming from the nurses' station would keep me awake. Sometimes, I would peer out my window from my bed, into the dark night, and watch the tiny specks of lights moving in the night sky. Maybe if I counted the planes flying, I would fall asleep.

In the wee hours of the morning, a team of attending doctors and interns entered my room for my daily check-up. If there were any concerns or questions, this was the time to discuss them. I mentioned my difficulty in sleeping, and said "Now I can relate to the movie 'Sleepless in Seattle'." They laughed at my joke and said a sleeping aid could help me sleep. That night I did not count planes.

The food at the Swedish Hospital was the best-tasting hospital food. I could order food up until 8 or 9:00 p.m. The meals included fresh fish caught right out of the ocean, fantastic desserts, even pizza or hamburgers. To pass the time, I would watch movies, read books, surf the internet, gaze out my window or talk on the phone. Occasionally, I would take my sketch pad and walk around the hospital floor looking for an interesting view to sketch.

On the day of my radiation procedure, I imagined magical rays going through my body zapping scleroderma left and right. When I returned to my room, I looked in the mirror and noticed I had a slight tan. I did not feel any different right away. A few hours later, I felt nauseous and tossed up my cookies. I munched on crackers and sipped chicken broth until I felt better. The chemotherapy came next and was administered intravenously. I experienced the same nauseous feeling. If the nausea became unbearable, there was always medication available. After five days of alternating radiation, chemotherapy and ATG, my body's immune system was eradicated and the stage was set for transplantation.

I did not have to wait long. The day my stem cells were implanted into my body is forever seared into my memory, June 12, 2000. This is my second birthday. The procedure itself is not complicated and as simple as a blood transfusion. It went quickly. Afterward, a medical attendant wheeled me back to my room. All the months of tests and preparation were over. Now it was a matter of waiting for my blood counts to climb and re-establish a brand new immune system. My buddy volunteer, Melissa Wagner, brought me a chocolate cake, my favorite, and balloons to celebrate my second birthday. We sang Happy Birthday and I was so blessed to have reached this point!

The following day, one of the nurses mentioned to me that my hair most likely would start falling out in clumps. She suggested, if I wanted, she could shave my head so I would not have to deal with the constant hair falling out. I said, "Sure, go right ahead. It is going to happen any way." When she finished, I walked over to the mirror to see the results. I looked like a Martian. There were lumps on my head I did not know existed. I went to my closet, pulled out one of the hats I brought for this occasion and pulled it over my head.

Sometimes, I would amuse myself to pass the time so I would not go stir crazy. I taped notes with drawings on my door that said "Gone fishing", "Went to climb Mt. Rainier, be right back" or "Caution: Patient turning into werewolf." I contemplated all the things I would do when I got better. My dad stopped by to visit every day. By the fourth week, I could not escape the cabin fever. I did not realize how much I would miss the outside air or the freedom to leave the building.

The two attending female doctors in charge of my care were great. Toni was a tall, slender brunette with almond-colored eyes and shoulder-length dark brown hair. Betty was petite with crystal blue eyes and short, blond hair. They both did a superior job monitoring my health throughout my stay in the hospital.

During my recuperation, I had a urinary catheter in place to prevent unnecessary walking to the bathroom. Bed rest and staying off my feet was important at this time. Out of all the procedures, this was the most uncomfortable procedure I experienced during my hospitalization. I was relieved once it was removed.

I experienced one strange side effect when my legs began to retain fluid and took on the appearance of tree trunks. I had to keep my legs elevated and took medication to encourage urination, ridding my body of excess fluid. After a few days, the swelling went down and my legs looked normal again.

Once my condition stabilized, the doctors mentioned releasing me at the end of my third week. Unfortunately, the night before my release, I developed a slight temperature, which postponed my discharge and forced me into isolation until my temperature returned to normal. I was not a happy camper and wanted so desperately to leave.

During my last week, my dad let me know that he was packing and getting ready to return to Arizona. He had to get back home. I could never thank him enough for all his help and support. His departure coincided with my daughters getting out of school for summer break. I knew they could take over as caregivers. I was thrilled to see them and sad to see my dad leave.

Chapter XV

Blissful Reunion

Before my daughters' arrival, I spoke to the nurse in charge of caregiving and explained my daughters would be taking over as my caregivers for the remaining month. She said as long as my daughters were mature and responsible, they could handle my care upon my discharge. They also were required to attend the caregiving classes. Since Natalie was 14 years old and Megan was 12, I knew they were independent and self-sufficient and could handle the caregiving.

The school year ended in late June and Natalie graduated from grammar school. Donna did a great job providing a safe and loving home for my daughters. She made arrangements for my daughters to fly up to Seattle. Before I knew it, they were headed to Seattle. I was still hospitalized when their plane touched down in Seattle. I was fortunate that the transplant coordinator in charge of volunteers, had a couple, Karen and David Hopkins, meet my daughters at the airport and drive them to the Pete Gross House apartment building. Since the flight was an evening arrival, I waited until the following day to see Natalie and Megan. We spoke by phone that night and could not wait to see each other.

The next morning, after what seemed like an eternity, my two daughters walked into my room with Karen and David. It was a great reunion to finally be together. We hugged and laughed all the while holding back tears. I looked over to Karen and David standing back and smiling at the scene before them. We shook hands and introduced ourselves to each other. This was my first time meeting Karen and David. Karen had brown, chin length, straight hair, coifed in a bob and hazel colored eyes. David was tall, broad built, with salt and pepper hair and possessed an easy-going nature. I felt a good connection with them and sensed these were good and kind hearted people.

My daughters were startled by my strange new appearance. We kidded around and I reassured them I was their mother. Finally, they sat down and we caught up on all the latest news from the last two months. Natalie showed me pictures of herself from her 8th grade graduation, in her gown, holding flowers, surrounded by my family. Before our visit ended, Karen asked if it would be okay to check in on Natalie and Megan and show them around town. I thought it was a fantastic idea since I was still recuperating in the hospital. I was grateful that Karen had the foresight to realize my daughters would be bored waiting for my discharge from the hospital. Just as she promised, Karen stopped by the apartment and took them to the mall and movies.

In the meantime, Natalie and Megan enrolled in the caregiving classes and learned all the procedures and techniques required for my care. Just in time, because the doctors determined that my condition was stable enough for me to go home.

On the day of my discharge, I was given instructions and a list of signs to watch for, such as an increase in temperature or infection. The discharge nurse also gave me a list of important names and phone numbers to call in case of an emergency. I packed my belongings, medications and medical supplies. It was a festive day and I felt like the luckiest person in the world. It just so happened I was discharged on the 4th of July. I was bursting with excitement to finally be out of my confinement! The hospital personnel did a wonderful job providing me with medical care, but I was glad to breathe the fresh air.

My daughters came to get me at the hospital and together we went back to our apartment. That evening we watched the fireworks from the rooftop along with other tenants in our building. It was a double celebration. There was so much to be thankful for. I was alive. My daughters were with me. I was surrounded by good people and I had a second chance at life! We listened to the music playing in unison with the exploding fireworks and watched the sparks trickling down onto Lake Washington. In that moment, I knew the true meaning of happiness and contentment.

After the fireworks ended, we returned to our apartment. My daughters joked with me about my new look, and we laughed at my bald head. They developed a schedule where they took turns caring for me. They did a brilliant job keeping house, cooking and attending to my needs. I could not have been more proud of them.

One day I had to stop by the manager's office, so I took the elevator down to the lobby. I entered the elevator and observed a young couple with luggage and baby items, such as a stroller, stuffed animals and toys. They smiled weakly and said hello. It was common to see new tenants arriving or patients and families leaving. Sometimes we would ask about each other's progress. My intuition told me not to ask since the young couple's manner was quiet and solemn. I found out later their baby daughter had leukemia and passed away. Their story touched my heart and was a reminder of how fragile our lives were. On the other hand, there were many success stories of patients responding well to their treatment.

The remaining days were filled with trips to the clinic for blood draws. My blood counts kept climbing and I did not experience any adverse side effects. I developed what I call teenage acne on my face and a slight tan from the radiation. My face had the round moon shape from the steroids. I was conscientious about hand washing and used caution whenever I was around crowds. We prepared most of our meals at home to guarantee a sanitary preparation. Occasionally, we splurged and went out for dinner.

We found time for sightseeing in between doctor's appointments. My daughters loved Pike's Market with its numerous shops, restaurants, fresh flowers, seafood and boutiques. We rode the old trolley cars and took a tour of the underground city. I had more energy than I could remember. From the top of the Space Needle, we took in the spectacular view of the city one last time. Karen or Melissa would call or stop by and take Natalie and Megan out on the days I was not feeling up to par. I took naps and focused as much as possible on my recuperation. I could not believe how quickly the three months in Seattle had gone by. At first, the days dragged incessantly, but now, the end was in sight.

Chapter XVI

A New Beginning

At my last check-up, I met with Dr. Furst. He gave me a complete examination and great news; my condition was stable enough for me to go back home to Chicago. He gave me instructions to give to my doctors for follow-up care. It was important that I get re-immunized immediately and schedule an appointment with an oncologist who would continue to monitor my health. I thanked him and Gretchen profusely for everything they had done for me. The doctors and nurses, with their knowledge and expertise, gave me the opportunity to live a second life.

The last medical procedure required was the removal of

the double-line catheter. I was anxious because I did not know if it would hurt. The medical technician told me it would be quick and not to worry. He had performed this procedure numerous times. I braced myself, and with one quick motion, he pulled the catheter out. Within milliseconds, it was over! It was reminiscent to the severing of an umbilical cord. This was my last and final connection to the transplant. The technician applied a bandage over the small wound and told me it would heal and close by itself.

LIKE MONET

An exquisite catheter was implanted in me,
Hidden from view so no one could see,
Like Monet, a piece of art,
It dangled in place next to my heart.
A portal essential for medication and nutrition,
Was the link to medical attention,
I was dependent as an infant to a mother,
I'll admit from one friend to another,
I am glad my old life is over and done,
Because I am ready and eager to start a new one.

The night before we were scheduled to leave, Karen and David invited us over for dinner. We met the other dinner guests, David's daughter and Karen's father. Karen's father was great with my daughters and gave each one of them a gold dollar coin to keep for good luck. David entertained us with his jokes and kept us in stitches while Karen prepared dinner. The food was tasty and delicious. It was a special evening spent with the most kindhearted and generous people I have ever encountered in my life. We ate, drank and talked until it was time for us to go home. After meeting such thoughtful and caring people as Karen and David, who helped complete strangers feel at home in a strange city, this experience changed my outlook on humanity. I am convinced there are angels living on earth.

After dinner we hugged and said our farewells. David drove us back to our apartment. That evening, we packed our belongings and prepared ourselves for the flight to Chicago the next day. We had already cleaned the apartment and put everything back in its place. It was a bittersweet moment because this had become my second home.

The next morning we stacked our luggage outside the apartment. I stood in the doorway taking in the small, cozy apartment one last time. I pulled the door knob until I heard the locking mechanism click. It was the end of a chapter in my life and the beginning of a whole new life. I looked forward to going home. We said good bye to everyone we knew in the building, headed for the airport, and boarded the plane bound for Chicago.

Chapter XVII

Post-Transplant

The year is now 2008. It has been eight years since my transplant. The improvements were gradual and not so obvious the first year. The first thing I did when I returned to Chicago was make an appointment for my immunization shots. The ulcers on my fingers, elbows and ankles are now gone. My energy and stamina levels are better. My skin score improved from a 25 to a 1 or 2. My pulmonary function test showed an increase of 25%, from a 60 to 85. One of the tests performed on my digestive system showed increased activity, where prior tests showed flaccid muscular activity. I can chew and swallow food without choking or having to drink liquids. My hair grew back, a little thinner than before, but at least I have hair.

I am amazed at the tasks I am able to perform now. I can mow the lawn, shovel snow, walk up and down stairs, reach over my head, bend and touch the ground with my hand. I can plan outings and not worry about getting fatigued. My weight level had gone back up 110 pounds. Presently, my weight varies and dips down to 90 pounds but I am working on bringing that figure back up.

Some things did not change. I still have the physical traits common in scleroderma, the pinched nose and small mouth. My fingers are still contracted and I can't fully bend the joints in my knees. The distinct hypopigmentation (skin discolorations) on my face, chest and hands did not completely clear up. I've come to the conclusion that the outward physical appearance does not reflect the person that I am inside. My heart and brain are still the same. Most importantly, I am alive to witness my daughters mature into young ladies and attend college. I am content knowing my family has a solid foundation from which any dream is possible. I reached my goal and have stopped chasing the cure. I am glad to say my desperate search for doctors and treatments to halt this disease has ended.

I've gone back to Seattle several times since the SCT for long term follow-up physical exams. I have fond memories of my experience there and hope by sharing my experience others will feel a sense of hope and encouragement. Some people call this a cure. I choose to call it a medical miracle.

The stem cell transplant put my disease in remission and prolonged my life. We still have so much to explore and learn from this procedure. I believe we have touched the surface in the arena of stem cell transplantation. I look forward to the advancement and research in this field.

Conclusion

Scleroderma is derived from the Greek word sklerosis meaning "hard" and derma meaning "skin". It is an autoimmune disease, where collagen overproduces and skin (connective tissue) begins to harden. There are various types of this disease, localized, systemic and sine. In localized, only the outer skin is affected. In systemic, the outer skin and internal organs are affected. In sine, a person is affected internally, yet appears normal on the outside. For unknown reasons, the autoimmune system begins to attack itself. When the internal organs are affected with scleroderma, the hardening process causes problems such as diminished lung capacity, pulmonary hypertension, renal failure, heart failure and other maladies. The internal organs most affected include the lungs, digestive system, kidneys, heart, vascular system and even the brain.

The cause of scleroderma is unknown. There are several triggering factors, i.e., bacterial, environmental, chemical agents, genetic, compounded stress and/or trauma-induced. This disease mainly affects women. Hundreds of thousands of people all over the world are affected with scleroderma. Scleroderma can be difficult to diagnose. Once a diagnosis is confirmed, it is difficult to predict its course or treat because each person's symptoms vary from extreme to slightly affected. Life expectancy can range from one year or less to twenty plus years.

Presently, there is no cure. There are medications available to alleviate pain, treat the symptoms and slow down the progress of the disease. Medical research is the key to discovering the cause and cure for scleroderma and other autoimmune diseases. Hopefully, in my lifetime, I will witness this event.

Stem cell transplants have saved many lives and can be utilized to treat many diseases. This treatment is now available in many clinical studies throughout the United States. In order to participate in a study, a candidate must qualify based on the study's requirements. It is important to review the protocol and risks involved before making a decision to join a study. Doctors have studied the techniques and protocols of previous stem cell transplant studies and implemented changes or variations to the more recent studies.

A few doctors have promoted their stem cell transplant

study by using comparisons of their study to the one I was a participant. The climate of their presentation convinces potential candidates that their study has fewer risks and better results. All stem cell transplants have considerable risks with a possibility of death.

It is important that I tell my experience so others can decide what options are available to them and to dispel any misconceptions. In order to preserve the integrity of a study, participants are numbered and kept anonymous. This maintains the accuracy of a study and prevents participants from sharing information and duplicating responses to questions in follow-up clinical appointments. In the Seattle SCT study, participants were numbered and not allowed to contact one another. We were severely affected with scleroderma and diagnosed with a high risk of mortality. Current studies have lessened restrictions and requirements for potential candidates, thus assuring a higher success rate. Implementation of the SCT in an early diagnosis is also the key to a successful transplantation.

Stem cell transplantation is not a recent discovery. Bone marrow transplantation was discovered by Dr. E. Donnall Thomas, who was the first doctor to infuse patients with donor bone marrow in 1955. It was through his tenacity and research that we have what is known today as stem cell transplantation. The Fred Hutchinson Cancer Research Center, formerly known as The Fred Hutchinson Center, was founded in 1975 by Drs. William Hutchinson and. E. Donnall Thomas. The first hematopoietic stem cell transplant in the

United States was also performed at the Fred Hutchinson Cancer Research Center. In 1990, Dr. Thomas was awarded the Nobel Prize for his remarkable pioneering work on the first safe harvest and transplantation of bone marrow. To date, three Nobel Prizes have been awarded to researchers at the Fred Hutchinson Cancer Research Center.

Presently, more than 9,000 bone marrow and stem cell transplants have been performed at the Fred Hutchinson Cancer Research Center and its treatment partnership, the Seattle Cancer Care Alliance. The Fred Hutchinson Cancer Research Center is a renowned transplant center in the United States and in the world, and trains physicians from different countries. This knowledge and information is used to save the lives of tens of thousands of patients each year. More than 300 graduate and postdoctoral students are trained each year at the center by the most skilled and experienced doctors.

I am grateful to Dr. E. Donnall Thomas for his pioneering work that rescued my life and to the transplant team who performed my stem cell transplant at the Fred Hutchinson Cancer Research Center. I wish to honor all the patients who participated in prior studies so that others, including myself, could benefit and learn from these studies. It is through their generous gift that we have successful and improved treatments available.

My wish for those who have experienced the gift of a stem cell transplant is to enjoy a long and fruitful life. May your journey in this world continue through smooth and harmonious paths for many years and may your health continue to improve with each passing day.

Acknowledgments

A sincere and gracious thank you to everyone involved in my care and quest to find a cure.

Thank you to Dr. E. Donnall Thomas for his pioneering work in bone marrow transplantation.

To Drs. Richard Nash and Daniel Furst for their work and my acceptance into the stem cell transplant study.

To Dr. Michael Ellman for providing me with many years of expert medical treatment.

To Drs. Leona Holmberg, Tina Passarelli, Betty Stewart and the transplant team at the Swedish Hospital for their round-the-clock medical care during my treatment and recuperation.

To the medical personnel at the Fred Hutchinson Cancer Research Center for their outstanding medical care.

To the fantastic volunteers associated with the Seattle Cancer Care Alliance in Seattle, Washington.

To Donna and Mike Brennan for providing loving care to my children.

To Karen and David Hopkins for providing a second home to us.

To Patty Nykowski for accompanying and helping me get situated in Seattle, Washington.

To the Pete Gross House staff and management for making us as comfortable as possible throughout our stay.

To Pat Bravo and all my brothers and sisters in the Chicago Police Department, who without their assistance none of this would be possible.

And most of all to my family and friends, who without their relentless love and support, I could not have undergone this unbelievable experience.

www.ingramcontent.com/pod-product-compliance
Lightning Source LLC
Chambersburg PA
CBHW030950090426

42737CB00007B/560